I0813468

The Essential Earle Birney

The Essential Earle Birney

selected by Jim Johnstone

The Porcupine's Quill

Library and Archives Canada Cataloguing in Publication

Birney, Earle, 1904–1995
[Poems. Selections]
The essential Earle Birney / selected by Jim Johnstone.

Includes bibliographical references.
ISBN 978-0-88984-373-8 (pbk.)

I. Johnstone, Jim, 1978–, editor of compilation II. Title.

PS8503.I72A6 2014 C811'.54 C2014-900695-0

1 2 3 • 16 15 14

Published by The Porcupine's Quill, 68 Main Street, PO Box 160,
Erin, Ontario N0B 1T0. http://porcupinesquill.ca

 The portrait on page two is after a charcoal by Harold Town; the image is reproduced courtesy of Nancy Rahija and the Estate of Harold Town.

Represented in Canada by Canadian Manda.
Trade orders are available from University of Toronto Press.

We acknowledge the support of the Ontario Arts Council and the Canada Council for the Arts for our publishing program. The financial support of the Government of Canada through the Canada Book Fund is also gratefully acknowledged.

Canada Council for the Arts
Conseil des Arts du Canada

Table of Contents

7 Foreword

1940–1951

11 David
18 Vancouver lights
20 Anglosaxon street
22 The road to Nijmegen
24 Mappemounde
25 Canada: case history: 1945
26 From the hazel bough
27 Ulysses
28 Can. Lit.
29 Takkakaw Falls
31 Bushed

1952–1970

32 Ellesmereland
32 Ellesmereland II
33 Twenty-third flight
34 A walk in Kyoto
36 The bear on the Delhi road
38 El Greco: *Espolio*
40 Caribbean kingdoms
41 Cartagena de Indias, 1962
47 Epidaurus
49 Canada Council
50 Museum of man

1971–1987

51 first aid for poets
52 She Is
54 On her twenty-sixth
55 Fall by fury
59 coming back from the airport
60 Copernican fix
60 my love is young

61 About Earle Birney
63 Earle Birney: A Bibliography

Foreword

When Earle Birney published 'David' in *The Canadian Forum* in 1941, he was 37 years old. 'David' would go on to become the centrepiece of his first book, and its popularity was such that it was reprinted in both his second and third collections. Although he was a late starter, Birney would go on to write over twenty books of poetry as well as a myriad of short stories, radio plays and scholarly articles. But it was 'David' that became his most enduring work—a 200-line narrative poem that explores the mercy killing of the eponymous David after a fall from a mountain ridge. It was career-defining not only due to its ubiquity on the national stage—an argument could be made that it's the quintessential Canadian poem of the 20th century—but also, as Carmine Starnino writes in *Lazy Bastardism*: '[as] the poem [Birney] tried his entire career to defeat.'[1] Consequently, much of Birney's later work can be read as reactionary, writing against what A.J.M. Smith called 'the simple and unified narrative [of] "David".'[2]

The work that followed the publication of *David and Other Poems* (1942) is striking for both its prescience and its range. Birney was one of the foremost medieval literary scholars of his day, and several of his early poems incorporated Anglo-Saxon alliterative structures and diction. The most successful of these pieces, 'Anglosaxon street' and 'Mappemounde', were written during the Second World War and modernize Chaucerian cadences to articulate the social anxieties of the time. Birney was also a satirist, as can be seen in 'Twenty-third flight', and he sustained an interest in political irony, penning sequels to his poem 'Canada: case history: 1945' in 1973 and 1985. His other dominant poetic modes included travelogues ('A walk in Kyoto'), short lyrics ('From the hazel bough'), elegies ('Cartagena de Indias, 1962') and even concrete poems ('Canada Council').

---

1. Starnino, Carmine. *Lazy Bastardism*. Kentville, Nova Scotia: Gaspereau Press, 2012. Print.
2. Smith, A.J.M. 'A Unified Personality: Birney's Poems.' *A Salute to Earle Birney*. Special issue of *Canadian Literature* 30 (1966): 3–13. Print.

Foremost in Birney's poetic output stands 'Bushed', published in *Trail of a City and Other Verse* (1952), of which Northrop Frye wrote: 'that for the virtuosity of language there has never been anything like it in Canadian poetry.'[3] The pinnacle of Birney's existential lyricism, 'Bushed' examines the distortion of an unnamed trapper's soul due to isolation. Consider the following stanza:

> But the moon carved unknown totems
> out of the lakeshore
> owls in the beardusky woods derided him
> moosehorned cedars circled his swamps and tossed
> their antlers up to the stars
> then he knew   though the mountain slept   the winds
> were shaping its peak to an arrowhead
> poised

Teeming with menace, these lines capture Birney in mid-career, when his poetry was at its most nuanced and muscular. Along with 'David', 'The bear on the Delhi road', 'El Greco: *Espolio*', and 'Cartagena de Indias, 1962', 'Bushed' established Birney as one of the finest Canadian poets of the 20th century.

In *The Creative Writer* (1966), a collection of lectures that Birney prepared for the CBC, the poet asserted: 'Living art, like anything else, stays alive only by changing.'[4] His poetry reflects this statement—Birney made significant edits to many of his most canonized pieces throughout his career, despite criticism. Birney's *Selected Poems* (1966) can be seen as something of a sea change in this regard: nearly every poem in the book was reformatted to remove punctuation, with the notable exception of 'David'. The grammatical and typographical changes that began in *Selected Poems* were refined further in *The Collected Poems of Earle Birney* (1975), and it's from

---

3. Frye, Northrop. *The Bush Garden: Essays on the Canadian Imagination*. Toronto: Anansi, 1971. Print.
4. Birney, Earle. *The Creative Writer*. Toronto: Canadian Broadcasting Corporation, 1966. Print.

this point forward in Birney's bibliography that the poems in this volume have been chosen.

The transformation of Birney's work in the 1960s and 1970s was accompanied by a reevaluation of his poetics. He addressed this in the preface to *Ghost in the Wheels: Selected Poems* (1977), when he wrote: 'I should say at the start that I don't any longer like the words "poet", "poems", etc. They've developed pretentious connotations. I prefer "maker" and "makings". They mean the same but the texture's plainer, oatmeal, not manna.'[5] Far from being an idiosyncrasy, the removal of rhetorical and syntactic markers in Birney's work corresponds with his desire for 'indefinitely delayed communication'[6]. While this was considered unnecessary at the time, today the ambiguity created by Birney's editorial changes charges the general reader with discovery, and rewards open-ended interpretations of his poems by creating enjambments that mimic song.

Despite the fact that the poems chosen in *The Essential Earle Birney* are retroactively stylized in a manner that unifies them, chronology is significant when considering Birney's output. A meticulous record-keeper, the poet kept track of the date of initial composition and completion of all his work. This record is helpful when tracing Birney's development in relation to his contemporaries, and the poems in this volume are arranged chronologically to allow for juxtaposition while also establishing the trajectory of Birney's writing life. Some of his most radical work, written during a period of linguistic experimentation that saw him align with the avant-garde in the late 1960s, benefit from comparison with poems of that era.

While Birney never abandoned his experimental instincts, he devoted much of his last 20 years to writing a sequence of

---

5. Birney, Earle. *Ghost in the Wheels: Selected Poems*. Toronto: McClelland & Stewart, 1977. Print.
6. Wilson, Milton. 'Poet Without a Muse.' *A Salute to Earle Birney*. Special issue of *Canadian Literature* 30 (1966): 14–20. Print.

extraordinary love poems for his partner, Wailan Low. Represented here by 'She Is', 'On her twenty-sixth', 'coming back from the airport' and 'my love is young', his final poems are remarkable for their directness, honesty and deceptive simplicity. A synthesis of Birney's playful nature and technical mastery, the poems for Wailan distill the youthful exuberance of their relationship in intensely personal terms. More than anything else he wrote, these lyrics capture Birney unguarded, and they provide a fitting epilogue to one of the most diverse bodies of work of the 20th century.

—Jim Johnstone

David

I

David and I that summer cut trails on the Survey.
All week in the valley for wages, in air that was steeped
In the wail of mosquitoes, but over the sunalive week-ends
We climbed, to get from the ruck of the camp, the surly

Poker, the wrangling, the snoring under the fetid
Tents, and because we had joy in our lengthening coltish
Muscles, and mountains for David were made to see over,
Stairs from the valleys and steps to the sun's retreats.

II

Our first was Mount Gleam. We hiked in the long afternoon
To a curling lake and lost the lure of the faceted
Cone in the swell of its sprawling shoulders. Past
The inlet we grilled our bacon, the strips festooned

On a poplar prong, in the hurrying slant of the sunset.
Then the two of us rolled in the blanket while round us the cold
Pines thrust at the stars. The dawn was a floating
Of mists till we reached to the slopes above timber, and won

To snow like fire in the sunlight. The peak was upthrust
Like a fist in a frozen ocean of rock that swirled
Into valleys the moon could be rolled in. Remotely unfurling
Eastward the alien prairie glittered. Down through the dusty

Skree on the west we descended, and David showed me
How to use the give of shale for giant incredible
Strides. I remember, before the larches' edge,
That I jumped a long green surf of juniper flowing

Away from the wind, and landed in gentian and saxifrage
Spilled on the moss. Then the darkening firs

And the sudden whirring of water that knifed down a fern-hidden
Cliff and splashed unseen into mist in the shadows.

III

One Sunday on Rampart's arête a rainsquall caught us,
And passed, and we clung by our blueing fingers and bootnails
An endless hour in the sun, not daring to move
Till the ice had steamed from the slate. And David taught me

How time on a knife-edge can pass with the guessing of fragments
Remembered from poets, the naming of strata beside one,
And matching of stories from schooldays... We crawled astride
The peak to feast on the marching ranges flagged

By the fading shreds of the shattered stormcloud. Lingering
There it was David who spied to the south, remote,
And unmapped, a sunlit spire on Sawback, an overhang
Crooked like a talon. David named it the Finger.

That day we chanced on the skull and the splayed white ribs
Of a mountain goat underneath a cliff-face, caught
On a rock. Around were the silken feathers of hawks.
And that was the first I knew that a goat could slip.

IV

And then Inglismaldie. Now I remember only
The long ascent of the lonely valley, the live
Pine spirally scarred by lightning, the slicing pipe
Of invisible pika, and great prints, by the lowest

Snow, of a grizzly. There it was too that David
Taught me to read the scroll of coral in limestone
And the beetle-seal in the shale of ghostly trilobites,
Letters delivered to man from the Cambrian waves.

V

On Sundance we tried from the col and the going was hard.
The air howled from our feet to the smudged rocks
And the papery lake below. At an outthrust we balked
Till David clung with his left to a dint in the scarp,

Lobbed the iceaxe over the rocky lip,
Slipped from his holds and hung by the quivering pick,
Twisted his long legs up into space and kicked
To the crest. Then grinning, he reached with his freckled wrist

And drew me up after. We set a new time for that climb.
That day returning we found a robin gyrating
In grass, wing-broken. I caught it to tame but David
Took and killed it, and said, 'Could you teach it to fly?'

VI

In August, the second attempt, we ascended The Fortress,
By the Forks of the Spray we caught five trout and fried them
Over a balsam fire. The woods were alive
With the vaulting of mule-deer and drenched with clouds all the morning,

Till we burst at noon to the flashing and floating round
Of the peaks. Coming down we picked in our hats the bright
And sunhot raspberries, eating them under a mighty
Spruce, while a marten moving like quicksilver scouted us.

VII

But always we talked of the Finger on Sawback, unknown
And hooked, till the first afternoon in September we slogged
Through the musky woods, past a swamp that quivered with frog-song,
And camped by a bottle-green lake. But under the cold

Breath of the glacier sleep would not come, the moonlight
Etching the Finger. We rose and trod past the feathery
Larch, while the stars went out, and the quiet heather
Flushed, and the skyline pulsed with the surging bloom

Of incredible dawn in the Rockies. David spotted
Bighorns across the moraine and sent them leaping
With yodels the ramparts redoubled and rolled to the peaks,
And the peaks to the sun. The ice in the morning thaw

Was a gurgling world of crystal and cold blue chasms,
And seracs that shone like frozen saltgreen waves.
At the base of the Finger we tried once and failed. Then David
Edged to the west and discovered the chimney; the last

Hundred feet we fought the rock and shouldered and kneed
Our way for an hour and made it. Unroping we formed
A cairn on the rotting tip. Then I turned to look north
At the glistening wedge of giant Assiniboine, heedless

Of handhold. And one foot gave. I swayed and shouted.
David turned sharp and reached out his arm and steadied me,
Turning again with a grin and his lips ready
To jest. But the strain crumbled his foothold. Without

A gasp he was gone. I froze to the sound of grating
Edge-nails and fingers, the slither of stones, the lone
Second of silence, the nightmare thud. Then only
The wind and the muted beat of unknowing cascades.

VIII

Somehow I worked down the fifty impossible feet
To the ledge, calling and getting no answer but echoes
Released in the cirque, and trying not to reflect
What an answer would mean. He lay still, with his lean

Young face upturned and strangely unmarred, but his legs
Splayed beneath him, beside the final drop,
Six hundred feet sheer to the ice. My throat stopped
When I reached him, for he was alive. He opened his grey

Straight eyes and brokenly murmured 'over… over.'
And I, feeling beneath him a cruel fang
Of the ledge thrust in his back, but not understanding,
Mumbled stupidly, 'Best not to move,' and spoke

Of his pain. But he said, 'I can't move… If only I felt
Some pain.' Then my shame stung the tears to my eyes
As I crouched, and I cursed myself, but he cried
Louder, 'No, Bobbie! Don't ever blame yourself.

I didn't test my foothold.' He shut the lids
Of his eyes to the stare of the sky, while I moistened his lips
From our water flask and tearing my shirt into strips
I swabbed the shredded hands. But the blood slid

From his side and stained the stone and the thirsting lichens,
And yet I dared not lift him up from the gore
Of the rock. Then he whispered, 'Bob, I want to go over!'
This time I knew what he meant and I grasped for a lie

And said, 'I'll be back here by midnight with ropes
And men from the camp and we'll cradle you out.' But I knew
That the day and the night must pass and the cold dews
Of another morning before such men unknowing

The way of mountains could win to the chimney's top.
And then, how long? And he knew… and the hell of hours
After that, if he lived till we came, roping him out.
But I curled beside him and whispered, 'The bleeding will stop.

You can last.' He said only, 'Perhaps... For what? A wheelchair,
Bob?' His eyes brightening with fever upbraided me.
I could not look at him more and said, 'Then I'll stay
With you.' But he did not speak, for the clouding fever.

I lay dazed and stared at the long valley,
The glistening hair of a creek on the rug stretched
By the firs, while the sun leaned round and flooded the ledge,
The moss, and David still as a broken doll.

I hunched to my knees to leave, but he called and his voice
Now was sharpened with fear. 'For Christ's sake push me over!
If I could move... or die...' The sweat ran from his forehead,
But only his eyes moved. A hawk was buoying

Blackly its wings over the wrinkled ice.
The purr of a waterfall rose and sank with the wind.
Above us climbed the last joint of the Finger
Beckoning bleakly the wide indifferent sky.

Even then in the sun it grew cold lying there... And I knew
He had tested his holds. It was I who had not... I looked
At the blood on the ledge, and the far valley. I looked
At last in his eyes. He breathed, 'I'd do it for you, Bob.'

IX

I will not remember how or why I could twist
Up the wind-devilled peak, and down through the chimney's empty
Horror, and over the traverse alone. I remember
Only the pounding fear I would stumble on It

When I came to the grave-cold maw of the bergschrund... reeling
Over the sun-cankered snowbridge, shying the caves
In the névé... the fear, and the need to make sure It was there
On the ice, the running and falling and running, leaping

Of gaping greenthroated crevasses, alone and pursued
By the Finger's lengthening shadow. At last through the fanged
And blinding seracs I slid to the milky wrangling
Falls at the glacier's snout, through the rocks piled huge

On the humped moraine, and into the spectral larches,
Alone. By the glooming lake I sank and chilled
My mouth but I could not rest and stumbled still
To the valley, losing my way in the ragged marsh.

I was glad of the mire that covered the stains, on my ripped
Boots, of his blood, but panic was on me, the reek
Of the bog, the purple glimmer of toadstools obscene
In the twilight. I staggered clear to a firewaste, tripped

And fell with a shriek on my shoulder. It somehow eased
My heart to know I was hurt, but I did not faint
And I could not stop while over me hung the range
Of the Sawback. In blackness I searched for the trail by the creek

And found it... My feet squelched a slug and horror
Rose again in my nostrils. I hurled myself
Down the path. In the woods behind some animal yelped.
Then I saw the glimmer of tents and babbled my story.

I said that he fell straight to the ice where they found him,
And none but the sun and incurious clouds have lingered
Around the marks of that day on the ledge of the Finger,
That day, the last of my youth, on the last of our mountains.

Toronto 1940

Vancouver lights

About me the night moonless wimples the mountains
wraps ocean land air and mounting
sucks at the stars The city throbbing below
webs the sable peninsula The golden
strands overleap the seajet by bridge and buoy
vault the shears of the inlet climb the woods
toward me falter and halt Across to the firefly
haze of a ship on the gulf's erased horizon
roll the lambent spokes of a lighthouse

Through the feckless years we have come to the time
when to look on this quilt of lamps is a troubling delight
Welling from Europe's bog through Africa flowing
and Asia drowning the lonely lumes on the oceans
tiding up over Halifax now to this winking
outpost comes flooding the primal ink

On this mountain's brutish forehead with terror of space
I stir of the changeless night and the stark ranges
of nothing pulsing down from the beyond and between
the fragile planets We are a spark beleaguered
by darkness this twinkle we make in a corner of emptiness
how shall we utter our fear that the black Experimentress
will never in the range of her microscope find it? Our Phoebus
himself is a bubble that dries on Her slide while the Nubian
wears for an evening's whim a necklace of nebulae

Yet we must speak we the unique glowworms
Out of the waters and rocks of our little world
we conjured these flames hooped these sparks
by our will From blankness and cold we fashioned stars
to our size and signalled Aldebaran
This must we say whoever may be to hear us
if murk devour and none weave again in gossamer:

These rays were ours
we made and unmade them   Not the shudder of continents
doused us   the moon's passion   nor crash of comets
In the fathomless heat of our dwarfdom   our dream's combustion
we contrived the power   the blast that snuffed us
No one bound Prometheus   Himself he chained
and consumed his own bright liver   O stranger
Plutonian   descendant   or beast in the stretching night—
there was light

1941

Anglosaxon street

Dawndrizzle ended   dampness steams from
blotching brick and   blank plasterwaste
Faded housepatterns   hoary and finicky
unfold stuttering   stick like a phonograph

Here is a ghetto   gotten for goyim
O with care denuded   of nigger and kike
No coonsmell rankles   reeks only of cellarrot
attar of carexhaust   catcorpse and cookinggrease
Imperial hearts   heave in this haven
Cracks across windows   are welded with slogans
There'll Always Be An England   enhances geraniums
and V's for Victory   vanquish the housefly

Ho! With climbing sun   march the bleached beldames
festooned with shopping bags   farded flatarched
bigthewed Saxonwives   stepping over buttrivers
waddling back wienerladen   to suckle smallfry

Hoy! With sunslope   shrieking over hydrants
flood from learninghall   the lean fingerlings
Nordic nobblecheeked   not all clean of nose
leaping Commandowise   into leprous lanes

What! After whistleblow!   spewed from wheelboat
after daylong doughtiness   dire handplay
in sewertrench or sandpit   come Saxonthegns
Junebrown Jutekings   jawslack for meat

Sit after supper   on smeared doorsteps
not humbly swearing   hatedeeds on Huns
profiteers politicians   pacifist Jews

Then by twobit magic to muse in movie
unlock picturehoard or lope to alehall
soaking bleakly in beer skittleless

Home again to hotbox and humid husbandhood
in slumbertrough adding sleepily to Anglekin
Alongside in lanenooks carling and leman
caterwaul and clip careless of Saxonry
with moonglow and haste and a higher heartbeat

Slumbers now slumtrack unstinks cooling
waiting brief for milkmaid mornstar and worldrise

Toronto 1942

The road to Nijmegen*

December my dear on the road to Nijmegen
between the stones and the bitten sky
was your face

Not yours at first
but only the countenance of lank canals
and gathered stares
(too rapt to note my passing)
of graves with frosted billy-tins for epitaphs
bones of tanks beside the stoven bridges

and old men in the mist
hacking the last chips
from a boulevard of stumps

These for miles and the fangs of homes
where women wheeled in the wind
on the tireless rims of their cycles
like tattered sailboats,
tossing over the cobbles

and the children
groping in gravel for knobs of coal
or clustered like wintered flies
at the back of messhuts
their legs standing like dead stems out of their clogs

Numbed on the long road to mangled Nijmegen
I thought that only the living of others assures us
the gentle and true we remember as trees walking
Their arms reach down from the light of kindness
into this Lazarus tomb

So peering through sleet as we neared Nijmegen
I glimpsed the rainbow arch of your eyes
Over the clank of the jeep
your quick grave laughter
outrising at last the rockets
brought me what spells I repeat
as I travel this road
that arrives at no future
and what creed I can bring
to our daily crimes
to this guilt
in the griefs of the old
and the graves of the young

---

* Nijmegen was in 1944–5 the town at the tip of the Canadian salient in Holland, connected with rearward troops by a single much-bombed highway. The area had been the scene of tank battles, artillery duels, air raids, buzz-bomb and V-2 rocket attacks. It had also been denuded of trees, coal and foodstocks by the retreating Germans. The winter was in all Europe one of the coldest of the century.

Mappemounde

No not this old   whalehall can whelm us
shiptamed gullgraced   soft to our glidings
Harrows that mere more   which squares our map
See in its north   where scribe has marked *mermen*
shore-sneakers who croon   to the seafarer's girl
next year's gleewords   East and west *nadders*
flamefanged bale-twisters   their breath dries up tears
chars in the breast-hoard   the brave picture-faces
Southward *Centegrande* that   sly beast who sucks in
with whirlwind also   the wanderer's pledges
That sea is hight Time   it hems all hearts' landtrace
Men say the redeless   reaching its bounds
topple in maelstrom   tread back never
Adread in that mere   we drift to map's end

Hospital Ship El Nil, *Atlantic 1945*

Canada: case history: 1945

This is the case of a high-school land,
dead-set in adolescence;
loud treble laughs and sudden fists,
bright cheeks, the gangling presence.
This boy is wonderful at sports
and physically quite healthy;
he's taken to church on Sunday still
and keeps his prurience stealthy.
He doesn't like books, except about bears,
collects new coins and model planes,
and never refuses a dare.
His Uncle spoils him with candy, of course,
yet shouts him down when he talks at table.
You will note he's got some of his French mother's looks,
though he's not so witty and no more stable.
He's really much more like his father and yet
if you say so he'll pull a great face.
He wants to be different from everyone else
and daydreams of winning the global race.
Parents unmarried and living abroad,
relatives keen to bag the estate,
schizophrenia not excluded,
will he learn to grow up before it's too late?

Ottawa

From the hazel bough

I met a lady
    on a lazy street
hazel eyes
    and little plush feet

her legs swam by
    like lovely trout
eyes were trees
    where boys leant out

hands in the dark and
    a river side
round breasts rising
    with the finger's tide

she was plump as a finch
    and live as a salmon
gay as silk and
    proud as a Brahmin

we winked when we met
    and laughed when we parted
never took time
    to be brokenhearted

but no man sees
    where the trout lie now
or what leans out
    from the hazel bough

Military Hospital, Toronto 1945 / Vancouver 1947

Ulysses

Make no mistake sailor the suitors are here
    and the clouds not yet quiet
Peace the bitchy Queen is back
    but a captive still on shelter diet
The girl of your heart has been knitting long
    the boy-friends have arms there may be a riot
Go canny of course but don't go wrong
    there's no guarantee of an epic ending
Your old dog Time prone on the dungpile
    offers the one last whick of his tail
while you amble by not daring to notice
    and the phony lords grow fat on your ale

Soldier keep your eye on the suitors
    have a talk with your son and the old hired man
but the bow is yours and you must bend it
    or you'll never finish what Homer began

Toronto 1946

Can. Lit.

(or *them able leave her ever*)

since we'd always sky about
when we had eagles they flew out
leaving no shadow bigger than wren's
to trouble even our broodiest hens

too busy bridging loneliness
to be alone
we hacked in railway ties
what Emily* etched in bone

we French&English never lost
our civil war
endure it still
a bloody civil bore

the wounded sirened off
no Whitman wanted
it's only by our lack of ghosts
we're haunted

Spanish Banks, Vancouver 1947 / 1966

---

* Emily Dickinson

Takkakaw Falls

Jupiter   Thor   how he thunders!
High in his own cloud somewhere
smashes
explodes on her upslant ledges
arcs out foaming
falls fighting—
o roaring cold down-geyser—
falls
falls gyring   flings
rain rainbows like peacock flights
vaulting the valley
His own gale rends him
heads off spray-comets
that hurl from her taut cliff
shreds even his cataract core
juggles it
struggles—holds?
falls
ho
like Woden
Zeus
down
terrible the bolt of him
(writhing past firs
foamdrowned to skeletons)
the hissing iced-nebulae whirl of him
crashes
batters unstayable
batters bullthroated
life-lunging
Tak
ka
kaw
batters the brown
throbbing thighs of his mountain

Out of the mist meekly the stream

Milk-young he mewls in naked-green moss
bruise-purple boulders
Slickens to slope   pours
silt-turbulent through pine   races
whole to the Yoho   coils
with Columbia   wanders
the ocean tundra   climbs
by sunladders slowly to
storm
glacier
down to the
spawning
thunder

1950

Bushed

He invented a rainbow but lightning struck it
shattered it into the lake-lap of a mountain
so big his mind slowed when he looked at it

Yet he built a shack on the shore
learned to roast porcupine belly and
wore the quills on his hatband

At first he was out with the dawn
whether it yellowed bright as wood-columbine
or was only a fuzzed moth in a flannel of storm
But he found the mountain was clearly alive
sent messages whizzing down every hot morning
boomed proclamations at noon and spread out
a white guard of goat
before falling asleep on its feet at sundown

When he tried his eyes on the lake   ospreys
would fall like valkyries
choosing the cut-throat
He took then to waiting
till the night smoke rose from the boil of the sunset

But the moon carved unknown totems
out of the lakeshore
owls in the beardusky woods derided him
moosehorned cedars circled his swamps and tossed
their antlers up to the stars
then he knew   though the mountain slept   the winds
were shaping its peak to an arrowhead
poised

And now he could only
bar himself in and wait
for the great flint to come singing into his heart

Wreck Beach 1951

Ellesmereland

Explorers say that harebells rise
from the cracks of Ellesmereland
and cod swim fat beneath the ice
that grinds its meager sands
No man is settled on that coast
The harebells are alone
Nor is there talk of making man
from ice cod bell or stone

1952

Ellesmereland II

And now in Ellesmereland there sits
a town of twenty men
They guard the floes that reach to the pole
a hundred leagues and ten
These warders watch the sky watch them
the stricken hills eye both
A mountie visits twice a year
and there is talk of growth

1965

Twenty-third flight

Lo as I pause in the alien vale of the airport
fearing ahead the official ambush
a voice languorous and strange as these winds of Oahu
calleth my name and I turn to be quoited in orchids
and amazed with a kiss perfumed and soft as the *lei*
Straight from a travel poster thou steppest
thy arms like mangoes for smoothness
o implausible shepherdess for this one ageing sheep
and leadest me through the righteous paths of the Customs
in a mist of my own wild hopes
Yea though I walk through the valley of Immigration
I fear no evil   for thou art a vision beside me
and my name is correctly spelled
and I shall dwell in the Hawaiian Village Hotel
where thy kindred prepareth a table before me
Thou restorest my baggage   and by limousine leadest me
to where I may lie on coral sands by a stream-lined pool

Nay but thou stayest not?
Thou anointest not my naked head with oil?
Thou shepherdess of Flight Number Twenty-three only
thou hastenest away on long brown legs to enchant
thy fellow-members in Local Five of the Greeters' Union
or that favoured professor of Commerce mayhap
who leadeth thee into higher courses in Hotel Management
O nubile goddess of the Kaiser Training Programme
is it possible that tonight my cup runneth not over
and that I shall sit in the still pastures of the lobby
whilst thou leadest another old ram in garlands past me
and   bland as papaya   appearest not to remember me?
And that I shall lie by the waters of Waikiki   and want?

Honolulu 1958

A walk in Kyoto

all week   the maid tells me   bowing
her doll's body at my mat   is Boys' Day
also please Mans' Day   and gravely
bends deeper   the magnolia sprig in my alcove
is it male   the old discretions of Zen
were not shaped for my phallic western eye
there is so much discretion
in this small bowed body of an empire
(the wild hair of waterfalls combed straight
in the ricefields   the inn-maid retreating
with the face of a shut flower)   i stand hunched
and clueless   like a castaway in the shoals of my room

when i slide my parchment door to stalk awkward
through lilliput gardens framed & untouchable
as watercolours   the streets look much as everywhere
men are pulled past on the strings
of their engines   the legs of boys
are revolved by a thousand pedals
& all the faces are taut & unfestive as Moscow's
or Toronto's   or mine

Lord Buddah help us all there is vigour enough
in these islands & in all islands reefed & resounding
with cities   but the pitch is high   high as the ping
of cicadas (those small strained motors concealed
in the propped pines by the dying river) & only male
as the stretched falsetto of actors mincing the roles
of kabuki women   or female only as the lost heroes
womanized in the Ladies' Opera—
where in these alleys jammed with competing waves
of signs in two tongues & three scripts
can the simple song of a man be heard?

by the shoguns' palace   the Important Cultural Property
stripped for tiptoeing schoolgirls   i stare
at the staring penned carp that flail
on each others backs to the shrunk pools edge
for the crumb this non-fish tossed
in this the Day's one parable
or under that peeling pagoda the 500 tons
of hermaphrodite Word?

at the inn i prepare to surrender again
my defeated shoes to the bending maid   but suddenly
the closed lotus opens to a smile & she points
to where   over my shoulder   above the sagging tiles
tall in the bare sky & huge as Gulliver
a carp is rising   golden & fighting
thrusting its paper body up from the fist
of a small boy on an empty roof   higher
& higher   into the endless winds of the world

1958

The bear on the Delhi road

Unreal   tall as a myth
by the road the Himalayan bear
is beating the brilliant air
with his crooked arms
About him two men   bare
spindly as locusts   leap

One pulls on a ring
in the great soft nose   His mate
flicks   flicks with a stick
up at the rolling eyes

They have not led him here
down from the fabulous hills
to this bald alien plain
and the clamorous world   to kill
but simply to teach him to dance

They are peaceful both   these spare
men of Kashmir   and the bear
alive is their living   too
If   far on the Delhi way
around him galvanic they dance
it is merely to wear   wear
from his shaggy body the tranced
wish forever to stay
only an ambling bear
four-footed in berries

It is no more joyous for them
in this hot dust to prance
out of reach of the praying claws
sharpened to paw for ants
in the shadows of deodars
It is not easy to free
myth from reality
or rear this fellow up
to lurch   lurch with them
in the tranced dancing of men

Srinagar 1958 / Île de Porquerolles 1959

El Greco: *Espolio*

The carpenter is intent on the pressure of his hand

on the awl   and the trick of pinpointing his strength
through the awl to the wood   which is tough
He has no effort to spare for despoilings
or to worry if he'll be cut in on the dice
His skill is vital to the scene   and the safety of the state
Anyone can perform the indignities   It's his hard arms
and craft that hold the eyes of the convict's women
There is the problem of getting the holes exact
(in the middle of this elbowing crowd)
and deep enough to hold the spikes
after they've sunk through those bared feet
and inadequate wrists he knows are waiting behind him

He doesn't sense perhaps that one of the hands
is held in a curious gesture over him—
giving   or asking   forgiveness?—
but he'd scarcely take time to be puzzled by poses
Criminals come in all sorts
as anyone knows who makes crosses
are as mad or sane as those who decide on their killings
Our one at least has been quiet so far
though they say he talked himself into this trouble
a carpenter's son who got notions of preaching

Well here's a carpenter's son who'll have carpenter sons
God willing   and build what's wanted
temples or tables   mangers or crosses
and shape them decently
working alone in that firm and profound abstraction
which blots out the bawling of rag-snatchers
To construct with hands   knee-weight   braced thigh
keeps the back turned from death

But it's too late now for the other carpenter's boy
to return to this peace before the nails are hammered

Point Grey 1960

Caribbean kingdoms

Flowers live here as easily as air
They hang from power lines   they grow on light
A scalloped leaflet lying on a stair
will puff pink buds   and root itself in stone—
The animal hunts by day or pads within the night

The waxy jasmine   Indian arum   red mimosa
tangle unbruised   thigh to alien thigh
the dark Ashanti Blood   the yellow roses
keep peace beneath a prism sun—
White men alone the rainbow world deny

Stubborn as coral the crimson flowers rise
The torch plant towers higher than a man
Each dawn hibiscus gaze with newmade eyes
and cereus nightly stars the jungle roof—
The other kingdom rules what roosts it can

Petal and bract outdo the stir of sky
Their silent cockatoos in every park
preen and are fed without the need to fly
Coldly they nourish birds of heat   and shelter
all bony forms that cry before the dark

Still souls of butterflies the orchids poise
about the flaming trees and are not singed
Lilies turn spiders into spirit   dragons to toys
The Passion Flower lifts its crucifix unmanned—
Only the worlds of blood on suffering are hinged

When all the life of sound has milled
to silence I think these vines will find
a way to trumpet green and purple still
and jacarandas ring their bells down ruined streets—
Our kingdom comes and goes with mind

Mona, Jamaica 1962

Cartagena de Indias, 1962

Ciudad triste, ayer reina de la mar
(Heredia)

Each face its own phantom
its own formula of breed and shade
but all the eyes accuse me back and say

There are only two races here:
we human citizens
who are poor but have things to sell
and you   from outer space
unseasonable   our one tourist
but plainly able to buy

This arthritic street
where Drake's men and Cole's ran
swung cutlasses   where wine and sweet blood
snaked in the cobble's joints
leaps now in a sennet of taxi horns
to betray my invasion
All watch my first retreat
to barbizans patched from Morgan's grapeshot
and they rush me
three desperate tarantula youths
waving Old Golds unexcised

By an altar blackened
where the Indian silver was scratched away
in sanctuary leaning   on lush cool marble
I am hemmed by a conga drum-man in jeans
He bares a brace of Swiss watches
whispers in husky Texan

Where gems and indigo were sorted
    in shouting arcades
    I am deftly shortchanged
and slink to the trees that lean
and flower tall in the Plaza
    nine shoeboys wham their boxes
    slap at my newshined feet

Only in the Indio market
mazed on the sodden quais
I am granted uneasy truce
Around the ritual braidings of hair
the magical arrangements of fish
the piled rainbows of rotting fruit
I cast a shadow of silence
    blue-dreaded eyes
    corpse face
    hidalgo clothes
    tall one   tall as a demon
    pass O pass us quickly

Behind me the bright blaze of patois
    leaps again

I step to the beautiful slave-built bridge
and a mestiza girl
    levels Christ's hands at me
    under a dangling goiter

Past the glazed-eyed screamers of *dulces*
swing to a pink lane
where a poxed and slit-eyed savage
    pouts an obscenity
    offering a sister
    as he would spit me
    a dart from a blowpipe

Somewhere there must be another bridge
from my stupid wish
to their human acceptance
but what can I offer—
my tongue half-locked in the cell
of its language—other than pesos
    to these old crones of thirty
    whose young sink in pellagra
    as I clump unmaimed
    in the bright shoes
    that keep me from hookworm
    lockjaw and snakebite

It's written in the cut of my glasses
I've a hotelroom all to myself
with a fan   and a box of Vitamin C
It can be measured
in my unnatural stride
that my life expectation
is more than forty
especially now that I'm close to sixty

older than ever bankrupt Bolívar was
who sits now in a frozen prance
high over the coconut trays
quivering on the heads
    of three gaunt mulatto ladies
    circling in a pavane of commerce
    down upon spotlit me

Out of the heaving womb of independence
Bolívar rode   and over the bloody afterbirth
into coffee and standard oil
    from inquisitional baroque
    to armed forces corbusier

He alone has nothing more
to sell me

I come routed now scuffling
through dust in a nameless square
treeless burning deserted
come lost and guiltily wakeful
in the hour of siesta
at last to a message

to a pair of shoes
in a circle of baked mud
worn out of shape one on its side
For a second I am shaken by panic
heat? humidity? something has got me
the shoes are concrete
and ten feet long

the sight of a plaque calms
without telling me much

En homenaje de la memoria de
LUIS LOPEZ
se erigió este monumento
a los zapatos viejos
el día 10 de febrero de 1957

Luis Lopez? Monument to his old shoes?
What??? There was nothing else
and the square was asleep

Back through the huckster streets
the sad taxi men still begging with horns
to the one bookstore

Si señor   *Luis Lopez el poeta*
Here is his book
Unamuno praised it   *si si*
You have seen *los zapatos?*   Ah?
But they are us, *señor*
It was about us he wrote
about Cartagena where he was born
and died   See here this sonnet
always he said hard things about us
Said we were lazy except to make noise
and we only shout to get money
ugly too, backward... why not?
it is for a poet to say these things
Also he said *plena*—how say it?—
plena de rancio desaliño
Full of rancid disarray!
Si, Si, but look at the end, when old
he come to say one nice thing
only one ever about us
He say we inspire that love a man has
for his old shoes—*entonces*
we give him a monument to the shoes

I bought the book   walked back
sat on the curb happier than Wordsworth
gazing away at his daffodils

Discarded queen   I thought   I love you too
Full of rancid disarray
city like any city
full of the stench of human indignity
and disarray of the human proportion
full of the noisy always poor
and the precocious dying
stinking with fear   the stale of ignorance
I love you first for giving birth
to Luis Lopez   suffering him
honouring him at last
in the grand laconic manner
he taught you

—and him I envy
I who am seldom read by my townsmen

Descendants of pirates   grandees
galleyslaves and cannibals
I love the whole starved cheating
poetry-reading lot of you   most of all
for throwing me the shoes of deadman Luis
to walk me back into your brotherhood

Colombia 1962 / Greece 1963

Epidaurus

Taking the baths for their nerves
anxious Corinthian ladies
no doubt complained to the attendants
about the noise
        pedlars
                                        MUSSELLLS!
                                        FIGgggs!
                        donkeys
                        foot pilgrims
                        weekend chariots
all that shoving and braying
past Aesculapius' own temple
into the great new eyesore of a showplace
and the brawling out again
with torches into the night

Now everything's been put right
                        'the visitor is offered
                        every convenience   easy access
                        unlimited parking   refreshments
                        at the   Tourist Pavilion
                        also a quick & comfortable
                        getaway'
and the season lasts only six weeks

After twenty-five centuries
something is also being done
about the wildflowers
flagrantly widening the cracks
in even the best seats

Everybody however
still waits to
hear the
pin
dr
o

p

Greece 1963

Canada Council

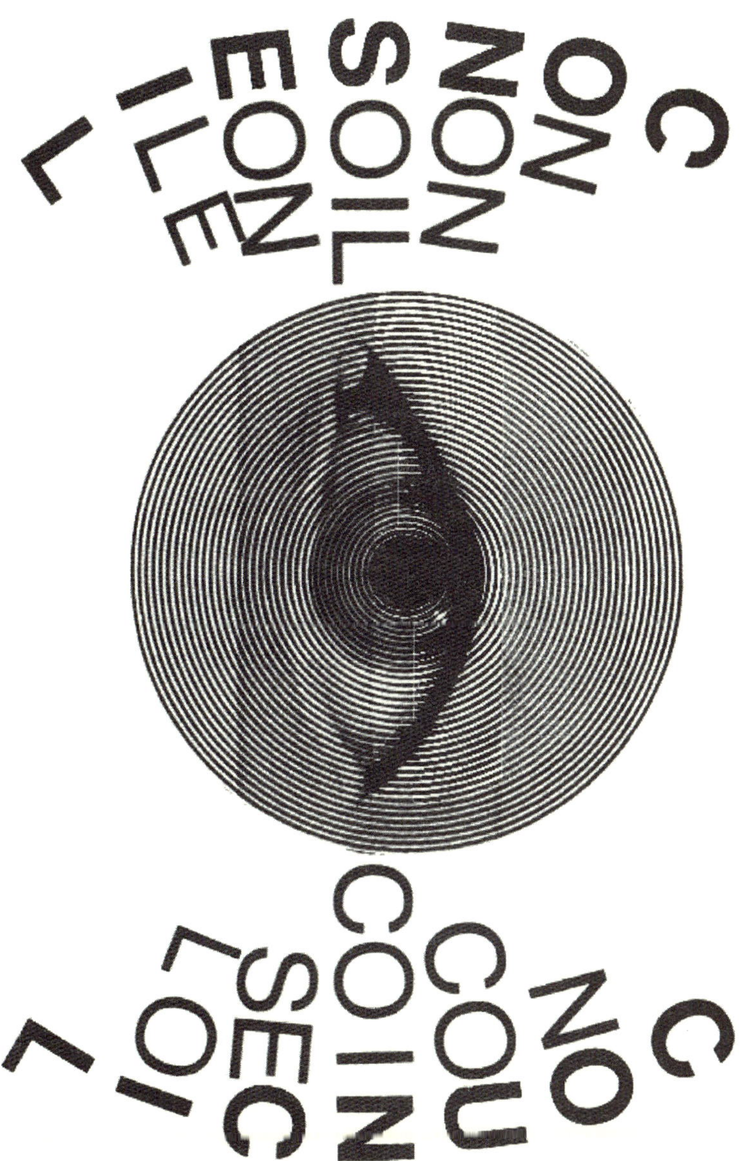

Ottawa 1967

Museum of man

the trustful curator has left me alone
in the closed wing of the aboriginal section

what's here?
3000 spears from arnhemland
waiting for a computer
to calculate their principle of balance

but what's in those wooden drawers?
i peek—sheeeez! shrunken heads
from new guinea
& dozens upon dozens
of twelve-inch penis sheaths

i'm going to lock doors
plant spears at windows
& try on everything for size

Adelaide 1968

first aid for poets

✦
d d
✦
e e
✦
i e
t
d n
h
ob es
e
m o
e ibs t
s t e i
i u
d fo mosq
T E
O B
arcs fing
t ✦ ✦ e
✦
c r
h s
e o
d f
tyb poet
h r
e y

Victoria, B.C. 1971

She Is

(for wailan, on her 24th birthday)

she is
a little spruce tree
fresh every way
herself
like a dawn

when warm winds come
she will move
all her body
in a tremble of light

but today she stands
in magical stillness
she has clasped
all my falling flakes
from the round of her sky
and wished them
into her own
snowtree

through the cold time
she holds me
with evergreen
devotion
she bears up my whiteness

o so light may i press
letting each needle
grow in her own
symmetry
for i am at peace
in her form
after whirling
and faithful to all
her curves

but when warm winds come
we must stir from this trance
she will lift living arms
to the sun's dance

i will slide then
in a soft caress
of her brown sides
and my falling will end
somewhere in her roots

may my waters then
bring her strength only
help her hold trim
and evergreen her being
with suns and winds
for o many and many
and happiest years

Treehouse, Uxbridge 1974

On her twenty-sixth

At six you folded paper boats
with nowhere to sail them down
except a tub in Chinatown

Sixteen you climbed into a dory
to heave through sloughs of English Lit
and came by a dying lake to sit

Then we shaped our own canoe
birch-delicate but strong
and big enough for two

Over the portage freed
we steer through rapids worth the battling
They flow to a living sea

Sit straight dear twenty-six
hold firm the blade you've made
Mine dips with yours however frayed

With luck and will we'll reach
at last some bronzed arbutus beach
From there you'll sail the world

Give my old paddle then a simple burning
Sift the ashes down
where the fish and weed are turning

  But today   sweet twenty-six
  rest your eyes from the current's shine
  loose your small palms from the coursing
  let them find mine.

January 1976

Fall by fury

Now was the season
summer so high and still
the birds in the circling woods
held all the tale

Past deserted nests I rose
through a world of web with swede-saw
severing
dropping
the black treebones
for the consummation of winter fire
O through the brace and embrace
of a hundred living arms I swung
gathering delight in my own ease
muscle and breath at a play of skill

I was climbing the tall beech
to prune dead limbs
that overhung the summer home
before some gale might hurl
a snag into glass

Each grasp tugged at the old zest
for a climb:
the rock-fort a year back
in Sri Lanka
and before in my sixties
up the yellow spines of Australia's Olgas ...
at fifty-eight in the cloudy Andes on the ribs
of Huayna Picchu at thirty
inching down English chalk on Lulworth cliffs
... twenty-one and over the icy necks
of the Garibaldis and before that
the cliffs of my teens ... Temple ...

Edith ... all the climbings
made in joy of the sport
and never with hurt to me or to others

as now to the topmost vault
of the beechtree's leaves I rose
to the flooding memories
of childhood
perched in my first treehouse
safe in its green womb

Where brittle branches had threatened
a tunnel of light
shone up to me now
as i sat in the secrets of leaf
and smiled on the innocent roof
that hid my love preparing our noon-day meal

Shining ahead was the fortnight
given us here alone by our friends
to swim with the small fish in their pond
read and doze in the sun
hide in the sumac to watch
the little fox by their den
or to work with hands on wood
and heart on words
rhythms already shaping themselves
in the piney air
this first of the mornings

So I threw the last snag down
and the locked saw after
turning and shifting my grips
to descend to Wailan
when something   my Hubris
some Fury of insect wind and sting
drove its whining hate at my eye
One hand unloosed
convulsive to shield
and I slipped
forever from treetops

Caught in a yielding chair of air
I grasped and grasped
at a speeding reel
of branches half-seized
and wrenched away
by the mastering will
of the earth
The next bough surely—
my hard mother
crushed me limp in her stone embrace
stretched me still
with the other limbs
laid my cloven hip and thigh
with those I had cleft

And that was a world
and two summers ago
yet still in the night I reach
for holds eluding my clutch
till the moment comes
when the Furies
relent

I catch and cling
swoop
alight on friendly ground

and run again on two good feet
over the grass of dream

Toronto 1977

coming back from the airport

the flat's not real
a room restored
in a period museum
exact but unconvincing
i do not believe the tv
will turn on

your small slippers
poke from under the chesterfield
something arranged
by a slick director
they do not move
lacking the brown feet
which were human
with minute calluses

i water the chrysanthemum
silent as a photograph
nothing drinks
the armchair
stiff with air

only the bed
grows & is heard
twice as big
petrified with tousling
& yet an imitation too
a stuffed animal

nothing warm under the fur
no
body

July 1977

Copernican fix

the sun never sets
it's we who rise
& think
to shine

1983

my love is young

my love is young & i am old
she'll need a new man soon
but still we wake to clip and talk
to laugh as one
to eat and walk
beneath our thirteen-year-old moon

good moon   good sun
that we do love
i pray the world believe me
& never tell me when it's time
that i'm to die
or she's to leave me

Toronto 1973–1986

About Earle Birney

Alfred Earle Birney was born in Calgary, Alberta, in 1904. An only child, he learned to read by reciting selections from the Bible, John Bunyan's *Pilgrim's Progress*, and newspapers like *The Family Herald* and *Weekly Star*. As a young man, he worked numerous odd jobs, including brief stints with mosquito-control gangs and survey parties in the mountains. He was also a climber and his experiences in the Bow Valley above Banff ultimately led to 'David', one of his finest poems.

In 1922, Birney enrolled at the University of British Columbia where he earned his B.A. in English Literature in 1926, before completing an M.A. at the University of Toronto in 1927. He entered the doctoral program at the University of California at Berkeley in the fall of the same year, though he left to teach English at the University of Utah without having completed his degree. By this time he had become a Marxist-Leninist, and in 1934 he travelled to London on a Royal Society fellowship where he met Esther Bull, also a Marxist, whom he later married. Returning to Toronto in 1936, Birney completed his Ph.D. in Chaucerian irony at the University of Toronto, and was appointed as the literary editor of *The Canadian Forum*.

After the birth of his son, Bill, in 1941, Birney published his first book, *David and Other Poems* (1942), which bolstered his reputation when it was awarded the Governor General's Literary Award in Poetry. His next book, *Now Is Time* (1945), written while he served overseas as a personnel officer in the Canadian Army, also received the Governor General's Literary Award in Poetry. During the war, Birney served in England, Holland and Belgium, and his experiences led to the comic military novel *Turvey* (1949), which became a bestseller and was awarded the Stephen Leacock Medal for Humour.

Birney accepted a position as a professor of English literature at the University of British Columbia in 1946, a post he held until 1965. He continued to write both poetry and prose, with a novel drawing on his Marxist activities in the 1930s, *Down the Long Table*, appearing in 1955. His collections of poetry during this period include *The Strait of Anian* (1948), *Trial of a City and Other Verse* (1952), *Ice Cod Bell or Stone* (1962), and *Near False Creek Mouth* (1964). Birney's time at the University of British Columbia is also notable for his development of the Department of Creative Writing. In 1967, he became the first writer-in-residence at the University of Toronto.

An avid traveller, Birney gave poetry readings in the United States, Latin America, Great Britain, France, Australia, New Zealand, Asia and Africa in the 1960s and 1970s. His *Selected Poems* appeared in 1966, and he was appointed as an Officer of the Order of Canada in 1970. Inspired by writers like bpNichol, Birney released two experimental collections of poetry in the early 1970s: *rag & bone shop* (1971) and *what's so big about GREEN?* (1973). In April 1973 he met Wailan Low, who would remain his partner until his death. She was the inspiration for a vivid sequence of love poems.

Writing in many genres in his final years, Birney produced the memoir *Spreading Time* in 1980, and his radio plays were collected as *Words on Waves* (1985). He was honoured with a Vancouver Lifetime Achievement Award in 1987, shortly before suffering a disabling stroke. His final book of poetry, *Last Makings* (1991), was compiled while he was cared for at Queen Elizabeth Hospital in Toronto. He died in 1995, at the age of 91.

Earle Birney: A Bibliography

POETRY

David and Other Poems (1942); *Now Is Time* (1945); *The Strait of Anian* (1948); *Trial of a City and Other Verse* (1952); *Ice Cod Bell or Stone* (1962); *Near False Creek Mouth* (1964); *Selected Poems: 1940–1966* (1966); *Memory No Servant* (1968); *pnomes jukollages & other stunzas* (1969); *The Poems of Earle Birney* (1969); *rag & bone shop* (1971); *The Bear on the Delhi Road* (1973); *what's so big about GREEN?* (1973); *The Collected Poems of Earle Birney* (1975); *Alphabeings and Other Seasyours* (1976); *The Rugging and the Moving Times* (1976); *Ghost in the Wheels: Selected Poems* (1977); *Fall by Fury & Other Makings* (1978); *Copernican Fix* (1985); *Last Makings* (1991); *One Muddy Hand: Selected Poems* (2006).

FICTION

Turvey (1949).
Down the Long Table (1955).
Big Bird in the Bush (1978).

NON-FICTION

The Creative Writer (1966).
The Cow Jumped Over the Moon (1972).
Spreading Time (1980).
Essays on Chaucerian Irony (1985).

DRAMA

The Damnation of Vancouver (1977).
Words on Waves (1985).